Designed by The Creator:

The Human Body and the

Innate Intelligence Within

Curtis Reynolds, D.C.

Copyright © 2020 Dr. Curtis M Reynolds

ISBN: 9798637798131

Dedication:

I would like to dedicate this book to my family. First, to my parents for raising me to know my Maker. Second, to my wife, for putting up with me and for giving birth to our 3 beautiful children. Lastly, to my siblings. All have taught me something that has lead me to where I am today. I'm especially grateful for my family. I love you all!

PREFACE

The Human Body is an amazing, intricate, beautifully designed work of art. Its elaborate design has baffled scientists for years. Even with new technology, advances in medicine, and other technological advances, we do not entirely understand it. The real question is, "How did this body come to be?". Is it by chance? Is it evolution? The purpose of this book is to discuss one essential fact; The Creator Designed the human body. Who Is The Creator? Some believe in Jesus or God, while others believe in a great spirit or Allah. The fact remains, The Creator designed it. No matter what your religious background is, you probably believe in a "Higher Power", a "Supreme Being". I believe His name is God. You may believe differently. It is irrelevant. The truth is that "we" believe that our body is designed by this "Higher Power" and if you do not believe it, I encourage you to read this book and decide for yourself if your body could have been created by any other means.

You may also be asking yourself, "What is Innate Intelligence?". Innate intelligence is the intelligence found within our bodies that requires no instruction and no outside influence. It simply knows what to do. This intelligence is innate, meaning: existing in, belonging to, or determined by factors present in an individual from birth: native; inborn; belonging to the essential nature of something or inherent; originating in or derived from the mind or the constitution of the intellect rather than from experience (Merriam-Webster Dictionary). The innate intelligence found within ourselves will simply blow your mind. I implore you, read this book, and you will have no doubt in your mind that The Creator designed you.

CHAPTER HEADINGS

1

The Creator

Who is "The Creator"? It matters not where He came from. It matters not where He is or what He is doing. What matters is that He is the ruler, the "Almighty," the "Supreme Being," "Allah," or "God." As stated earlier, I believe Him to be God. For now, I will call Him "The Creator." The Creator is the one with all power and all understanding. He is all-knowing and can perform any miraculous act He chooses. He is the one who created all things, living and not living on this great Earth.

He created the universe according to His will. He created this Earth with all of its glory. The mountains, the plains, the jungles, the deserts, the rivers, and oceans are all witnesses of His mighty power. With all of this power, He could create anything He chooses. The Earth did not need humans to survive. Humans need the Earth, an undeniable truth. Yet, we are here.

In theism, God is the creator and sustainer of the universe. In deism, God is the creator (but not the sustainer) of the universe. In pantheism, God is the universe itself. Theologians have ascribed a variety of attributes to the many different conceptions of God. Common among these are:

1. Omniscience – having infinite awareness, understanding, and insight; possessed of universal or complete knowledge.
2. Omnipotence – an agency or force of unlimited power
3. Omnipresence – present in all places at all times
4. Omnibenevolence – perfect kindness and generosity or goodness
5. Divine simplicity, and eternal and necessary existence.

Monotheism is the belief in the existence of one God or in the oneness of God. God has also been conceived as being incorporeal (immaterial), a personal being, the source of all moral obligation, and the "greatest conceivable existent".

There are many names for God, and different names are attached to different cultural ideas about who God is and what attributes He possessed. In the ancient Egyptian era of Atenism, possibly the earliest recorded monotheistic religion premised on there being one "true" Supreme Being and Creator of the Universe, this deity is called Aten. In the Hebrew Bible "He Who Is," "I Am that I Am," and the "Tetragrammaton" YHVH are used as names of God, while Yahweh and Jehovah are often used in Christianity as vocalizations of YHVH.

In Arabic and other Semitic languages, the name Allah, "Al-El," or "Al-Elah" ("the God") is used. Muslims regard a multitude of titular names for God. At the same time, in Judaism, it is common to refer to God by the titular names Elohim or Adonai. The latter of which is believed by some scholars to descend from the Egyptian Aten. In Hinduism, Brahman is often considered a monistic deity. Other religions have names for God, for instance, Baha in the Bahá'í Faith, Waheguru in Sikhism, and Ahura Mazda in Zoroastrianism. (http://en.wikipedia.org/wiki/God)

According to the Muslim faith, "Allah" is the personal name of the One true God. Nothing else can be called Allah. The term has no plural or gender. This shows its uniqueness when compared with the word god, which can be made plural, gods, or feminine, goddess. It is interesting to notice that Allah is the personal name of God in Aramaic, the language of Jesus, and a sister language of Arabic.

The One true God is a reflection of the unique concept that Islam associates with God. To a Muslim, Allah is the Almighty, Creator, and Sustainer of the universe, Who is similar to nothing, and nothing is comparable to Him. His contemporaries asked the Prophet Muhammad about

3

Allah; they believe the answer came directly from God Himself in the form of a short chapter of the Quran, which is considered the essence of the unity or the motto of monotheism. Found in chapter 112 which reads:

"In the name of God, the Merciful, the Compassionate. Say (O Muhammad) He is God the One God, the Everlasting Refuge, who has not begotten, nor has been begotten, and equal to Him is not anyone." (http://www.allah.org/)

The Creator is universally known and accepted to be The Almighty, The Master, Alpha and Omega, the Supreme Being. How do we know that He loves us? How can we know of his goodness and power personally? We know because He chose to bless us with the miracle of the human body. The Creator designed us in His image. The phrase "His image" could mean many different things and is up for interpretation to most. I believe this to mean that my body and His body are similar in design. I believe He chose to give us the same body that He has. To me, this means He loves me very much and wants me to be happy. It also means that He has many blessings in store for me and wants me to be like Him.

As a father, I have participated in the great creation of children. I am no "Supreme Being," but my children look up to me just the same. I am to give my children an example to look up to and follow. I do my best to make sure that they have all that they need. The Creator does the same for us. He provided all things on this earth for us. He wants us to have all that we need so that we can be happy.

As you have read, many different descriptions and beliefs about The Creator exist in the world today. But, I ask you to look at the similarities between these beliefs. Have you noticed that all of these religious sects believe in a Supreme Being? How is this possible? How can practically every religion, every continent, every civilization throughout history believe in a Supreme Being? Why do so many believe this? I believe it is because He is real.

Doesn't it make sense to have multiple witnesses or beliefs from multiple sources prove His existence? I believe it does. What did all of these groups, religions, sects, and civilizations have to gain from believing this way? Is it all just some form of control? Most religions, especially in existence as they are today, believe The Creator gave us the power of Free Will. The power to choose for ourselves. If that's true, what control would belief in a higher power truly have?

It's obvious to see in the world today that people are choosing what they want to do regardless of the religions and beliefs in the world. The beauty is we do have the ability to choose. You can choose to believe there is a Creator or not. It's your choice. No one can force you to believe it. To me, the debate is over. I have seen, experienced, and felt so much evidence that He is real. So much in fact that I cannot deny it. There is debate throughout the religions over details about Him, an obvious truth. But there is one constant that remains true throughout history and the majority of religions. That there is a Creator, a Supreme Being, and He created us, this earth, this universe, and everything in-between.

WHY?

2

Why The Human Body?

Why were we created to have this frame, this brain, these organs, this body? I believe, as stated before, that the human body is created in the "image" of The Creator. It says in the Holy Bible that man was created in His image (God's image). I believe this to mean that The Creator has a body just like mine. Just as I have a son that has a body similar to mine, I believe we all have a body similar to the Father of All. Does that make sense? I think it does. Consider this; who would be best at designing this body? A creator that has a similar body or one that does not? Also, if The Creator loves us so much and wants us to have everything He has, which He says in the Holy Bible is what He wants, wouldn't it make sense that He would want us to have a body like His also? I think so.

You may ask yourself; What if I don't have a perfect body? What if I was born without limbs, without organs, with

6

missing or "broken" parts? The beauty of your body is that The Creator made it unique for all of us. When you die, your body will be resurrected in its entirety, a "better resurrection" (Hebrews 11:35, The Holy Bible, King James Version). I believe this means you would have the whole body as you would imagine you would have if your body were perfected. Those born blind, mentally ill, without limbs, etc, would have their sight, their full brain capacity, and would have their hands, feet, arms, and legs returned to their body. Those that have had accidents happen that caused damage to body parts, loss of body parts, or have had parts removed, etc., will also have those parts restored. According to what I believe, The Creator says that He will "change our vile body, that it may be fashioned like unto His" (Phillipians 3:21, The Holy Bible, King James Version).

The human body is a very complex organism. As we know, there are so many things about the body that we still do not fully understand. We don't fully understand how the body does what it does when so-called "miracles" happen. Science cannot explain it. Even the brightest among us will admit that they do not knows all there is to know about the human body. It is simply too complicated. Why do you think that is? I believe it is because it is supposed to be; it was designed to be.

The Creator gave us something that we could study for a lifetime and barely understand the complexity of it. For example, it is estimated that there are 86 billion, that's 86,000,000,000, neurons in the brain creating a neural network of 528,165 miles of axons and dendrites to connect them! (Transmitting fibers in the brain: Total length and distribution of lengths. <aiimpacts.org>) Good

7

luck understanding all of what happens in those neurons and networks!

We are designed to be able to accomplish anything we set our minds too. As noted in history, many did not believe man was capable of building amazing structures, creating such incredible weapons, using such useful tools, modes of transportation, and more until they saw someone else do it. We have it in us to be AMAZING! Why? How? I believe it is because The Creator designed us.

He has given us the innate abilities we are born with. Some are born to excel in science, some physically, some the ability to understand, some to communicate, others to art, writing, music, and dance, etc. Whatever it is that you somehow felt destined to do, or felt is your "calling" in life, was inborn in your body and your brain. All of which were given to you by The Creator.

The Human Body is different from all other lifeforms on earth, yet has so many similarities. For example, did you know that an earthworm has as many genes as a human, sometimes more? Or that we share nearly 70% of gene codes with marine worms? (You Share 70% of Genes with this Marine Worm. <livescience.com >).

Is it a coincidence that many species on earth use the similar codes found in the human body? If you were The Creator, wouldn't you use what works as a good base for all other species, maybe alter it a little here, a little there, and a lot when necessary? As for the argument that the human body and the ape body are similar, of course they are. But the similarities we see and know of for 100% certainty still leave us around 4% different. This difference is a fact. According to the Chimpanzee Genome Project, Apes that are similar to us in many ways have 24 chromosomes, while humans have 23 chromosomes. This difference is also fact. The fact remains that there are still several species of apes on the earth and only one human species after thousands of years.

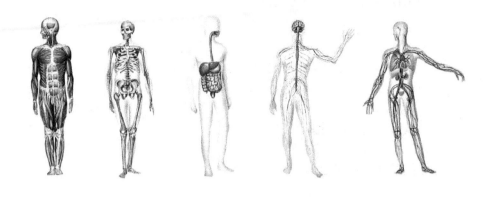

3

The Miracles Within

There are thousands of processes and interactions happening in the body all at the same time. It is of no surprise that there are many Miracles Within. This chapter will open your eyes to the many facts that are small miracles of the human body. When you think about them individually, you will have your mind blown by the amazing things that are happening all the time. When you think about them collectively, you will for sure recognize this is not just a mere chance but a Miracle Within.

The Nervous System:

1. Nerve impulses to and from the brain travel as fast as 170 miles per hour.[1]
2. The brain operates on the same amount of power as a 10-watt light bulb.[1]

3. The human brain cell can hold 5 times as much information as the Encyclopedia Britannica.[1]
4. The brain itself cannot feel pain.[1]
5. 80% of the brain is water.[1]
6. A trillion nerves are powering your memory. Studies have shown that after viewing 2,500 images for only 3 seconds, participants could recall if they had seen the images with 92 percent accuracy.[2]

The Skeletal System:

1. Babies are born with 300 bones, but by adulthood, the number is reduced to 206.[1]
2. In terms of compression strength, the femur bone of a person weighing 83kg with US size 11 feet could withstand the weight of 16,000 people standing on it at one time.[2]

The Renal and Urinary System:

1. Our kidneys filter all of the blood in our body about 400 times per day.[5]
2. The human bladder can stretch to hold about 400ml of urine.[5]
3. The kidney can clean more than 1 million gallons of water in a lifetime, which is more than enough to fill a small lake.[5]

The Circulatory System:

1. All red blood cells are replaced every 4 months.[1]
2. Your heart beats 100,000 times per day, pumping 5.5 liters per minute, which adds up to about 3 million liters of blood a year.[2]

3. The aorta is the size of a garden hose, while capillaries require 10 or more side by side to equal the size of a human hair.[1]
4. If all the DNA in your body were uncoiled, it would stretch out to about 10 billion miles, which is from Earth to Pluto and back.[2]

The Digestive System:

1. Stomach acid can dissolve metal.[2]
2. The largest internal organ is the small intestine.[1]
3. You get a new stomach lining every three to four days.[1]

The Integumentary System:

1. One human hair can support 3.5 ounces.[1]
2. Human hair is virtually indestructible.[1]
3. Feet have 500,000 sweat glands and can produce more than a pint of sweat a day.[1]
4. About 32 million bacteria call every inch of your skin home.[1]
5. Humans shed and regrow outer skin cells about every 27 days.[1]

The Respiratory System:

1. The surface area of a human lung is equal to a tennis court.[1]
2. Your left lung is smaller than your right lung to make room for your heart.[1]

The Endocrine System:

1. The body makes almost 30 different hormones.[4]

2. The pituitary gland is roughly the shape and size of a pea, which is impressive as it is the most important gland in the body. It regulates the other endocrine glands.[4]
3. The endocrine glands are all ductless. They secrete hormones straight into the bloodstream.[4]
4. The hypothalamus produces hormones that help to regulate how hungry or thirsty you are.[4]

The Muscular System:

1. It takes 17 muscles to smile and 43 to frown.[1]
2. You use 200 muscles to take one step.[1]

The Immune and Lymphatic System:

1. Fever releases white blood cells, increases metabolism, and stops certain organisms from multiplying.[3]
2. The immune system is a complex fighting system powered by five liters of blood and lymph. Lymph is a clear and colorless liquid that passes throughout the tissues of the body.[3]
3. If you're not getting more than five hours of sleep a night, your immune system can become depressed, just like you. This leaves you open to colds, flu, and infection.[3]
4. Exposure to sunlight is how your body naturally produces vitamin D. This helps ward off an array of bad things like depression, heart disease, and certain cancers.[3]
5. Laughter releases dopamine and other feel-good chemicals in the brain, all of which can help decrease stress.[3]

The Reproductive System:

1. The largest cell in the human body is the female egg, and the smallest is the male sperm.[1]
2. Every human spent about half an hour as a single cell.[1]
3. I believe the greatest miracle that comes from the reproductive system is children. I have 3 beautiful children and am grateful for the miracle they are. Shout out to Curtis, Kayla, and Leiana. Love you!

Other Interesting facts:

1. Your body is made up approximately 7 octillion atoms (that's 7,000,000,000,000,000,000,000,000,000 atoms).[2]
2. There are 37 trillion cells in your body.[2]
3. Cells in the inner lens of the eye, muscle cells of the heart, and the neurons of the cerebral cortex are the only cells that will be with you your entire life.[2]
4. Your eyes can distinguish between 2.3 and 7.5 million different colors.[2]
5. Your nose can differentiate between 1 trillion different smells.[2]
6. Your fingers can feel a ridge as small as 13 nanometers in size (7,500x smaller than the diameter of a human hair).[2]

References

1. Christina Laun, 100 Weird Facts About the Human Body.
2. Kate NG, Saturday, November 7, 2015, 18 Facts You Didn't Know About How Amazing Your Body Is, <indpendent.co.uk>.

3. Fun Facts About the Immune System, <healthline.com>.
4. Endocrine System Fun Facts, <biologydictionary.net>.
5. Interesting Facts About Urinary System, <medindia.net>.

4

The Gift of Senses

S enses are an incredible gift from our Maker. Imagine if you didn't have them. Most of us have imagined that happening and have thought about how sad it would be if we were missing one of our senses. What if you were missing several of them? Life would be pretty tough. I hope you can remember this chapter and think about it the next time you experience a great sensation such as the smell of a flower, the taste of your favorite food, the touch of a person you love, the sight of a sunset, or the sound of your favorite music.

Five senses are found in the human body; sight, smell, taste, hearing, and touch. Why would The Creator give us these senses? I believe it is because He loves us and wants us to experience the joy these senses can bring to our lives.

Senses are some of the most taken for granted gifts from our Creator. Let's not take them for granted anymore.

Sight: Many of us have decent to perfect vision. Many of us wear glasses. Many of us didn't start our life wearing glasses but eventually needed them. How often did you think, "I'm so grateful I can see without glasses.", before getting glasses? Probably only a few times. Several of you have had eye surgeries to either fix something wrong with your eye(s) or simply to enhance your vision. What was it like when you couldn't see out of one eye or both eyes? Not enjoyable, I know. I've had eye injuries, luckily none that ever required surgery, thank goodness.

Ever get an eye exam? They usually have to put drops in your eyes that dilate your pupils. Oftentimes you practically can't see anything. At that moment, if even for a brief second, you gain empathy for those that can't see. Following that experience, you gain an appreciation for your sight as soon as it returns. Gratitude for the gift of sight from your Creator.

Facts about your eyes and vision:

1. Your eyes can focus on 50 different objects every second.
2. Your eyes can distinguish approximately 10 million colors.
3. 80% of all learning comes through vision.
4. Eye muscles are the fastest contracting muscles in the body, contracting at speeds of 1/100th of a second.
5. Your iris, the colored part of your eye, has 256 unique characteristics.

Reference: 15 Facts about all-things eyes. March 26, 2019.
<versanthealth.com>

Smell: Smell is a fantastic gift. You know the feeling of having a stuffy nose and you can't smell anything? Others around you describe the scent of a flower, a food, a beverage, a place, and you can't smell it. You feel entirely bummed. You can see it, hear it, touch it, but you still feel entirely bummed because you can't smell it. Once your nose clears, you suddenly gain an appreciation for that gift.

Now don't get me wrong, there are bad smells too. Some of which can make you want to vomit. Yuck! When you're in that situation, you may wish you didn't have the gift of smell. But some smells can almost transport you to another place, another time even. Smell can help bring back memories or wake a person from being unconscious. Smells can warn you and inform you. We are truly blessed to be able to experience the smell of all The Creators creations. Next time you have a stuffy nose, hopefully, you can gain empathy for those that don't have this gift due to injury, deformity, or disease. Next time you smell something amazing, hopefully you think to yourself, "I'm so thankful to have the gift of smell!".

Facts about your nose and smell:

1. Your nose is the best air purifier and humidifier. It naturally humidifies the air you breathe and blocks germs and dust.
2. Humans are capable of detecting 10,000+ scents using our nearly 12,000,000 olfactory cells.

3. The sense of smell is the only sense connected to the hippocampus, the part of the brain responsible for memory formation.
4. Human babies know their mothers best by their scent.
5. Humans are capable of smelling feelings.

Reference: Baidya, Sankalan. April 13, 2014. 40 Facts About Human Nose. <factslegend.org>

Taste: Who loves food? I do! I don't even want to imagine what life would be like if I couldn't taste my food! Again, there are sometimes that we taste something disgusting and make you feel sick, but the opposite feeling, the feeling of "Yummy!" is far more common. It is a gift I know we take for granted.

Since smell is essential for taste, it's no wonder that when we have a stuffy nose, we can't taste practically anything. Not tasting something you know is delicious can drive you crazy! You see others eating it and exclaiming how delicious it is, and you don't get to experience that. Not fun.

As we know, taste buds are mostly responsible for what we taste. But our taste buds change with age. We develop tastes for things and disgust for others, and the older you are, the less taste buds you have. Maybe that's why you asked your grandparents, "How can you eat that!?!" when they were eating something you thought tasted gross. The Creator must know the pleasure of tasting something so amazing because He wanted us to be able to have that pleasure as well. How grateful I am for that! Again, I love food! Who's with me?!

Facts about your tongue and taste:

1. There are 10,000 or so taste buds in our mouths. 8,000 on our tongue and 2,000 in places like the inside of our cheeks, on the roof of the mouth, on the lips, and even under the tongue.
2. The tongue is the most flexible muscle in our body.
3. Every taste bud has somewhere between 50 and 100 taste sensing cells, and no individual cell is capable of tasting more than one taste.
4. Our mouth is home to 600 different types of bacteria, and a single drop of saliva can contain up to 1 million of those bacteria.
5. The tongue is the only muscle that works without any support from the skeleton. It is known as muscular hydrostat.

Reference: Baidya, Sankalan. June 23, 2014. 20 Interesting Human Tongue Facts. <factslegend.org>

Hearing: Anyone love the sound of music? My wife and kids love the movie, but I'm talking about the literal sound of music. Music can seem to penetrate the soul. It can move you, make you feel a certain way, touch your heart, bring peace to you, and so much more. I'll admit, some music has brought tears to my eyes and caused me to feel such incredible joy. Imagine if you couldn't hear that music you love so much.

Have you ever listened to the sound of the ocean, a waterfall, a thunderstorm, a river or brook? How about the sound of birds chirping, the wind blowing the trees, or the fantastic calls and sounds animals can create? Imagine if you couldn't. What a gift, right? To be able to hear the sounds of nature as given to us by The Creator is truly a blessing.

If you have experienced parenthood and you can hear, you might have been ecstatic when you listened to your child say "Momma" or "Dadda". Hearing is a blessing, indeed. Thanks to technology and several options out there, those that can't hear very well can usually find a solution to allow them to hear. For children born with ear issues, their hearing and ability to speak or understand speech is in jeopardy. Listen to your favorite song, your favorite sounds in nature, the heartbeat of a loved one, and express gratitude to The Creator for that gift!

Facts about your ears and hearing:

1. Your ear is also responsible for your sense of equilibrium or balance. [1]
2. There are 3 tiny bones in the inner ear; the malleus, incus, and stapes. [1]
3. Ears contain more than 20,000 hairs on average! This moves the wax out of the ear and protects the ear. [1]
4. Your ears never stop working, even when you're asleep. Your brain chooses to ignore the sounds while you're sleeping. [1]
5. The human audible range is approximately 20 Hz to 20,000 Hz, but best between 2,000-5,000 Hz. Any sound above 85dB is damaging to the ear. [2]

References:

1. June 23, 2017. Weird and Interesting Facts about the Human Ear. <belairhearingaids.com>

2. Lotter, Eugene. September 27, 2018. 20 Lesser Known Facts about Hearing. <health24.com>

Touch: The gift of touch has been felt by every person on this earth that has skin and proper functioning sensory nerves in their skin, starting from the moment you were born. (Technically speaking, most of our senses began working in the womb.) But from birth, we learn to recognize touch and how we like to be touched and adversely how we don't want to be touched. Touching others can create a connection, a bond. Being touched by the person or people you love can make you feel loved and special.

I love the gift of touch! I'm blessed to be able to use that gift to feel a persons spine and make adjustments to it as needed. Without the gift of touch, I wouldn't have my career. I am grateful for this gift. Some of you are missing the ability to touch due to missing limbs, deformities, injuries, and disease. There are prosthetics, but they cannot simulate the sense of touch, not yet.

Perhaps next time you see someone without the ability to touch or feel that connection on a regular basis, you will reach out to them another way. Perhaps you could simply smile at them and say hello and ask them how they're doing. Perhaps you could be their friend and allow them to connect emotionally. Perhaps you could be the blessing to someone that is out of touch.

Facts about touch:

1. Touch involves 2 brain pathways - one is physical; one is emotional. Touch is literally affected by

emotion. You feel different based on who is touching you and how.[1]

2. Touch is the first sense we develop. You feel touch starting at 3 weeks after conception. Yes, as an embryo in your mother's womb.[1] (Think of abortion. How sad is that?! They feel it!)
3. Touch can reduce your anxiety and lower blood pressure.[1]
4. There are approximately 5 million touch receptors in our skin, about 3,000 per fingertip.[2]
5. Touch stimulates the release of endorphins, which is why a mother's hug or kiss when you were injured literally made you feel better. [2]

References:

1. 5 Things You Never Knew About the Power of Touch. <powerofpositivity.com>
2. April 27, 2013. Interesting Facts on Touch. <elementsmassage.com>

The senses are amazing, aren't they?!?! Senses are more than just tasting, hearing, touching, smelling, or seeing something. Senses allow us to take in the world around us, create bonds with others, experience joy and comfort, peace and serenity, and so much more. Do you understand that your body is unique this way? That these senses are indeed a gift from The Creator? That He loves us so much that he wants us to be able to experience these senses to bring us joy and happiness?

Hopefully, this chapter has allowed you to gain more appreciation for these amazing gifts. Hopefully, you can use your senses to bless the lives of others that are missing some of these gifts. Maybe, instead of poking fun at someone, giggling, or staring at someone that is missing some of these gifts, we show love, kindness, and offer an emotional connection. It is a scientific fact that by doing this, you could change someone's life, or even save it. How wise The Creator is. He knows we need that connection and offers us many ways to make those connections with others. Starting right now, use the senses your Maker has given you and bless someone today.

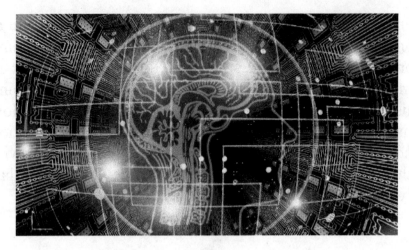

5

Innate Intelligence

Innate Intelligence is intelligence that is in the inborn body; native; inherent; as stated prior. You didn't put it there consciously; it was in you already. As soon as you were created, your body knew what to do. It's beautiful, isn't it? Isn't that amazing!?! I think it is! The egg from your mother knew to travel down the fallopian tube to the flesh of the uterine wall and attach to it. The sperm from your father knew to travel and find an egg with the singular purpose of fertilization of the egg. The first one there wins! Your mother didn't have to tell the egg to do that. Your father didn't have to tell his sperm how to swim, where to swim, and what to do when it got there. These processes happen without our conscious influence. This is part of our innate intelligence that started the process of your creation.

Once the sperm and egg meet, they join together to become one. The innate intelligence within those cells starts to work to divide, separate, differentiate, and so on. Some cells become nervous tissue, others heart and blood tissue, others bone and skin, and continues until your form starts to take place. Soon enough, your body was complete. All of these miracles, processes, and developments happen while in your mother's womb.

When you were born, you took a breath and probably cried. No one taught you how to breathe or cry, yet you did. Your mother possibly took you in her arms and as your mouth came close to her breast, your lips begin to move. Your mouth begins to shape into a circle to suckle for feeding. You nursed on your mother (or on a bottle), knowing how to get food and nourishment into your body. You did this without being taught how to do so.

I know what some of you are thinking, "Well, all creatures on earth do that. They procreate, they eat, they live, and die, mostly without learning how, so how are we any different?". And you're right. The beauty of knowing of a Creator is also knowing that He designed all living things on earth, every organism, every shape, every being. The Creator designed the trees, the plants, the grass, the fungi and algae, all living things. He even designed all non-living things. He is The Creator of All on this planet.

The Almighty, the Great Creator, provided the intelligence that exists within EVERY LIVING THING. Innate intelligence is one of several examples of that fact. How did the first organism know how to procreate, replicate, divide, eat, and so on without some outside influence? How? Chance? Because it simply "Had too."? I don't believe so. It received innate intelligence, instructions programmed into its cells. Those instructions were put there by someone. I call him my Maker.

Some of you are also struggling because your body is not "designed" well. You may be sick, suffering, born without a limb or worse. You may have been born with a disease, deformity, and so on. These diseases and deformities, weaknesses and infirmities, are examples of how outside influence can and will affect the innate intelligence within. These outside influences are usually some form of stress on the system affected. It could be emotional, physical, or chemical. All of these can change how the innate intelligence can work.

An interesting thing I learned in Chiropractic school is that it only takes pressure equal to approximately the weight of a dime on a nerve to affect its ability to transmit the information from brain to body part. How much does a dime weigh in your hand? Most can't even tell it's there because it's so light. We can feel it because our nerve endings are telling us that something is there but not because of its weight. This pressure on the nerve causes a change in that nerve's ability to send the information adequately.

This means that if the nerves going to your stomach are experiencing interference, you could experience acid reflux or unnecessary stomach contractions. You could have pressure on a nerve going to your hormone-producing glands. This means that your hormone glands may not be getting the message to secrete enough of a certain hormone, or that they are sending out too much. Here's a big one, what if the nerve going to your heart has interference, so it beats too much, too hard, or too fast? Nerve interference, or the interference of innate intelligence from brain to body, could be serious.

Interfering with innate intelligence is easy to do. There are many ways in which we do this every day. One way is with chemical stressors. We do this when we eat poorly, live in a toxic environment with high pollution, drink everything but water, and intoxicate our bodies with alcohol, smoke, drugs, and other toxins. Physical stressors also occur. We experience those when we fall while learning to walk/run/ride bike/climb or injuries when we play sports/trip/stub a toe/run into objects/quick jerking motions/accidents/etc. The stressors can also be emotional such as suffering loss, having anger, anxiety, hate, depression, and so on. All of these, which most of us do to ourselves regularly, affect the ability of our innate intelligence to do the job of keeping the flow of information from part to part, organ to organ, tissue to tissue, cell to cell. This disruption is an outside influence that adversely affects the innate intelligence flow.

Unfortunately, these disruptions can become permanent and passed onto our children. An instance of this is when a pregnant woman does drugs and alcohol while pregnant and the baby's development is altered. Another is when we suffer injury to our spine or another body part, and that part can no longer communicate at all, resulting in permanent loss of function.

How do we help innate intelligence do its job? How do we help the flow of information to keep going? How do we honor the blessing of this body that was given to us by The Creator? I'm going to provide a simple step-by-step process for you to follow. If you do, you will be showing The Creator that you are grateful for this gift of the Human Body, you will feel great, and you will be happier. As with most lifestyle changes, it won't be easy. Simple? Yes! Easy? Probably not. Let's begin.

6 STEPS TO A HEALTHIER YOU

and to
RELEASE
the
INNATE INTELLIGENCE WITHIN

1 Start with things you can control. You can control what you eat and drink. Start with eating a healthier, more balanced diet. Make sure you don't overeat or indulge too much on any one thing. Instead, you should eat a little of this and a little of that. As stated in many references in religious scriptures across several religions, we are to treat our bodies as a temple. We have been given all things on this earth for us to eat or use, but red meat and certain things are to be eaten sparingly according to most religious sects. It's a smart way to live. Eating a healthy balance of meats, vegetables, fruits, nuts, and more allows our bodies to have the best chance to get the nutrition it needs.

2 Try drinking nothing but water for several days. It will cleanse so many organs and tissues, hydrate dehydrated tissues, and more. It also provides a new lining for your stomach and entire digestive tract. The break from processing food will cause the soft tissues of your

digestive tract to shrink a little. Yep, even your stomach will shrink a little. Once you begin eating again, your stomach will get fuller faster. It will also help in filtering out toxins in your blood and kidneys. Your body will thank you with increased energy, weight loss, less joint pain, clearer skin, and so much more.

3 Get rid of those external toxins that you take into your bodies voluntarily. For many, this includes too much soda, coffee, tea, or other drinks. They may taste good, and occasionally be ok for you, but remember, "Too much of a good thing is a bad thing.". For many of you, this may be excessive alcohol consumption, smoking, or drugs. These may be addictions and require help from others, therapists, and friends to quit. Do it. Find a therapist, get a coach, join a group. Do what you can to rid yourself of these toxins in your life. If it's a vice like soda, coffee, tea, remember the water step above. If you're addicted to these drinks, I encourage you to reduce your intake right away. Are you addicted? Can you go days without one of those drinks? If you experience withdrawals such as body aches, headaches, or stress, your body is probably thirsty for water. Make the change. Your body will thank you.

4 Protect yourself from outside things that will adversely affect your innate intelligence. This protection process includes several things from washing your hands and proper hygiene to make sure you protect yourself by using condoms, gloves, and other protective measures when risk is high. There's no reason to jeopardize your health or that of another when there are easy ways to protect yourself and others. This is a serious step.

At the time of writing this section, March of 2020, we are dealing with a worldwide pandemic, COVID-19. This virus is serious and spreads mostly through respiratory droplets, as is the same with most viruses. We prevent it best with proper hygiene, i.e., washing hands, use sanitizer, wash your body daily, wash your clothes, brush your teeth, use mouthwash, etc. Most diseases throughout time were reduced and managed with hygiene. Protect this gift The Creator has given you and help protect others.

5 As a Doctor of Chiropractic, I have seen proof that physical changes can result in adverse effects on the flow of innate intelligence. I have seen infertile patients become fertile, digestive issues resolved, hormone balance achieved, and more simply by manipulating bones from a poor position back into their proper position. This repositioning, this manipulation, can relieve the pressure on the nerves that are causing those adverse effects. In short, visit a chiropractor today and see what misalignments you have that may be adversely affecting your flow and causing disease. It changed my life and may change yours.

6 Lastly, emotional stressors are difficult to deal with. Avoid those that treat you poorly, say negative things about you, or tear you down. Negativity can and often will lead to depression, anxiety, loneliness, and unhappiness. If necessary, you may need to search for new friends or join a help group. I recommend joining a church group with uplifting people. A therapist is also helpful in many instances to free you of these emotional stressors, and I highly recommend that you use one if necessary.

Innate Intelligence is a gift. We can use it to our benefit or we can abuse it and possibly destroy it. If we do too many negative things to our bodies, we can lose this precious gift. However, if we nurture it, feed it, and take care of it, the intelligence within us will continue to regulate our bodies and keep our bodies in optimum health.

You have probably experienced this in your life. As you eat junk regularly, you probably noticed a change in skin, digestion, clarity, and energy. When you ate healthily for a few days or even just one day, you probably noticed better skin, regularity with digestion, a clearer mind, and increased energy. If you have not had this change, I encourage you to start now. Start eating healthier, exercise, and take care of this amazing human body and the innate intelligence within. Do what you can to treat it with respect and express gratitude for it.

Are you

6

Sick or Healthy?

When your body is showing signs or symptoms, are you sick, or are you healthy? This is an important fact to know; When you are showing signs and symptoms of disease, you are HEALTHY! If your body did not show signs and symptoms of disease, you would be SICK! Do you understand the difference there? The purpose of this chapter is to help you understand the difference between these two words as it applies to your body.

Many in the health industry, especially big pharmaceutical companies, would have you believe that you are sick way more than you are healthy. These businesses and corporations don't make money on healthy people; they only make money on sick people. If everyone were healthy, they would go broke, not good for business. Let's look at this from the understanding that The Creator created our bodies. He gave us body systems that communicate with us to let us know when something is wrong, and frequently we know what it is or what it was that caused it.

<u>FEVERS</u>

Let's talk about one of my favorite symptoms of a healthy person that practically everyone in the world knows about and tries to alter as soon as it starts. Fevers are in response to, or preparation for, an invasion of bacteria or viruses. Fevers are a sign of a healthy individual who's body is doing what The Creator designed it to do. If we lower it right away, not only are we lowering our ability to prevent or kill the bacteria or virus, we are telling The Creator that we don't trust His design, we trust medicine.

Babies have fevers when teething to escalate body temperature outside of bacteria or virus range. Doing this stops bugs and viruses from coming into the breaking gums of the baby. Babies put a lot of things into their mouths that have bacteria and/or viruses on them so why do we lower the temperature? Because many in the health industry have convinced you that the innate intelligence provided by The Creator to your baby isn't good enough, you need to use drugs to lower that fever.

So you give your baby a fever-reducing drug. You notice the fever is down, and you congratulate yourself on lowering your baby's temperature and say you're doing a good job. The problem is that now that the fever is down, the bacteria and viruses now have the temperature they need to survive and multiply. Next thing you know, your child has a cold, flu, an ear infection, a digestive issue, and so on. It is the case for fevers throughout our lives.

We are convinced that it's a sign of sickness and that we must take a drug to bring our temperature down without ever asking why we're having the fever or considering that The Creator gave me this fever to fight off this bug. Can a fever be dangerous? Of course it can. In no way am I suggesting that you should let fevers run their course every time. What I am suggesting is that you learn safe levels of fevers and dangerous ones.

Dangerous, according to emedicinehealth.com, is 104-107. Have you ever let a fever get above 103, close to 104? Probably not. Have you ever let your child have a fever that high? Probably not. Why not? If it's not even dangerous, why lower the temperature? Why not trust in the design of The Creator? Having fevers means you are healthy! If you don't have a fever when you have a bug, then you are sick!

DIGESTION ISSUES

Second, let's look at digestive issues like acid reflux, indigestion, upset stomach, and diarrhea. Most are self-inflicted, meaning you ate something or drank something you shouldn't have, or you accidentally ingested a bacteria/virus. If you eat junk food daily, drink soda daily, and lay around, you will most likely experience many if not all of the symptoms listed above. So, are you sick or healthy? You are healthy! Meaning your body is telling you that you are doing something to it that is not good! Now, if you eat like that, drink like that, and do nothing and feel no signs or symptoms of disease, then you are sick! See how that works?

Now let's say you are experiencing those symptoms. Instead of changing something in your diet or exercise routine, you decide to cover up those symptoms with pills and syrups that reduce acid reflux, indigestion, upset stomach, and diarrhea. Now you do not have those symptoms anymore. Are you sick, or are you healthy? You are sick! You are now keeping the toxins and problems in your body instead of getting them out the way your body wants too. Why do you cover up those symptoms The Creator gave you to tell you something is wrong? We are taught by the majority of the healthcare industry and science that they have the answer to our problems, not The Creator. Doing this shows distrust in the design.

PAIN

Now I will discuss one of the biggest problems on earth that we in the healthcare field have been trying to fix or cover-up since time began, pain. We experience pain and discomfort in some form or fashion regularly. Sometimes it's a simple pain like a small pinch or little prick. Sometimes it's in our bodies, organs, or brain. Sometimes the pain can cause us to consider removing that part of the body entirely just to get rid of the pain.

As a Chiropractor, I treat people with pain every day. I'm so grateful for my chiropractic story. Here is my story of pain and how I allowed the innate intelligence within my body to flow and fix my pain.

It began with me at 22 years old. I was in pre-med and wanted to become a Pediatrician. I loved the idea of helping children. I still do! I was recently married and was in our apartment. I went to throw that tissue into the trashcan in the kitchen. As I bent over to throw the tissue away, I felt something happen in my lower back that caused me extreme pain. I couldn't move. I placed my hands on my knees and would not get back up into an erect position. I couldn't. My wife walked in and asked what happened. I explained that all I did was put a tissue into a trashcan.

Bent over, and in extreme pain, I went to the ER. They asked me how it happened and took x-rays. I explained the same story that I told my wife. Nothing out of the ordinary was found on the x-rays. They dismissed me with muscle relaxers and pain killers. For the next four days, I crawled to the bathroom and rested because the drugs caused such nausea and grogginess that all I could do was lay there. After the fourth day, I spoke to the referring physician's office. They prescribed other meds and a pain patch. Those didn't work either. I kept trying to cover up the pain that my innate intelligence was telling me something was wrong, but I trusted medicine.

Eventually, the pain lead me to try injection therapy, during which I had two epidural injections. Still no relief. The medical model failed me. The doctors said that the next step was surgery. Yep, surgery. Surgery for a 22-year-old in otherwise fantastic shape and health. They were proposing a $100,000 surgery, months of rehab, and potentially permanent damage to my spine and soft tissue. All of that just to get rid of the pain I had. A relative of mine told me of a chiropractor in my town. I never knew about chiropractic before. I didn't know what to expect, but I decided to give that a try. Please note, not once did any physician I had been treating with prior ever mention chiropractic care or physical therapy. Not EVER.

The chiropractor took x-rays and noticed misalignments and asked how it happened. I gave the same story. But he insisted that I hurt my back long ago and I should remember it. Then I recalled when I was kneeboarding at 12 years old and had a nasty wipeout over a big wave that caused significant back pain. It was so bad that those on the boat had to pull me out of the water. They had to lay me flat on the boat for the rest of the trip. My parents did what any good non-chiropractic parents would do. They gave me drugs to cover up the pain. Within a day or two, I was back to doing normal 12-year-old things. He explained that the knee boarding accident probably caused this damage. Since no significant issues were found, he considered me safe for spinal manipulation.

He placed me into a side-lying position to perform the correction. Just the positioning caused me to cry from the pain. He did one side, I heard "Pop, pop, pop!" and I felt some release, a reduction in discomfort. I rotated to the other side and again, "Pop, pop, pop!", and I felt more release and more decreased pain. I sat up. He said, "Stand up.". I said, "I can't stand up.", as I said that I stood up. To my surprise, 99% of my pain was gone. This was a miracle for me. To go from the worst pain in my life to practically none in just a few minutes was incredible. That's all it took. I was a believer in chiropractic, and that changed my life. He relieved the pressure, allowed the flow of information to return, and my innate intelligence took back the control it had before. The beauty is that I get to do this daily in my office. It's a great blessing to serve those in need. They have interference in the flow of innate intelligence within their bodies, and they are listening to it, coming in to fix the problem, not just cover it up. They are healthy, and my job is to keep them that way. If you are suffering from disc or joint problems and you don't have pain, you are sick!

(Please understand, I'm not against all meds. I believe it is okay to use a medicine in certain cases to cover up your symptoms as long as you address the cause of the symptom. For instance, if I broke my leg and went to the hospital for repair, I would gladly take meds to cover the pain while they change my anatomy back into its proper place and allow my body to do the rest. Yes, this is an extreme case, but you get the point. The same applies to my children. I'll give them meds as needed to relieve symptoms while addressing the cause of the symptom. I'm not completely against all meds. Some serious illnesses and ailments require meds regularly and are understandable to some degree. Sorry, I'm not sorry to the chiropractic purists out there that believe Chiropractic can fix everything. Remember, I was on my way to being a Pediatrician first.)

Hopefully, this chapter has opened your eyes and your mind to see how poorly we are treating our bodies every day. How we are not trusting the design The Creator has given us. We need to think about our signs and symptoms of disease that we are experiencing. Instead of covering up those signs and symptoms with drugs or medicine, perhaps we should think about why we have them. Why is my innate intelligence telling me that something is wrong? What did I do to cause it? What can I change to fix it?

Look for solutions, not quick fixes, or covering it up. Practically all OTC drugs cover up symptoms and don't fix anything, yet they fly off the shelves, and the companies that produce them make billions yearly. Quick facts about the U.S. that should help open your eyes.

FOLLOW THE $$$$$$$$$$$$$$$$!

We spend more than any other country in the world on healthcare. 16.9% of our GDP, according to the Organization for Economic Cooperation and Development, OECD Health Statistics, July 2019. Other countries average is 8.8%. The next closest country is 12.2%.

Average Americans spend $10,586 per year, nearly twice the world average, according to the Organization for Economic Cooperation and Development, OECD Health Statistics, July 2019.

Since 1997, prescription drug use has increased by nearly 90% while the population has only increased by almost 20%, according to Quintiles IMS, 2017 Consumer Reports.

Despite all of this spending, and the fact that we are approximately 5% of the world population yet consume nearly 45% of the prescription drugs in the world, we rank poorly compared to other countries in health, infant mortality, and more. Check out these facts.

Out of 169 Countries studied, we are ranked number 73 in overall health according to the Bloomberg Global Health Index.

We suffer nearly twice as many cases of Congestive Heart Failure, Asthma, and Diabetes as compared to the comparable country average, according to the Peterson-Kaiser Health System Tracker.

We are the #1 country in Infant Mortality (more babies die here in the US than all other developed nations). At nearly 6 deaths per 1,000 live births as compared to the comparable country average of 3.4, according to the Peterson-Kaiser Health System Tracker. We are even ranked lower than some 3rd World countries!!

How is this possible? How come we are not a healthier nation when we spend more on healthcare than any other country and consume more medications than any other country by far? Because we are a SICK nation! We are not Healthy! We are broke and on meds. Meds are not the answer. Change this in your life. Make changes to become Healthy today. Start small and work your way up to significant changes. Show The Creator that you are going to do what you can to help keep the body He has given you in the best shape you can. Start now! You got this!

7

"The Power that made the body, heals the body."

B.J. Palmer

W hat happens when you get injured? What happens when you damage an organ or tissue and need healing? Do you tell your body to repair the damaged organ or tissue? Do you send out instructions on how to fix the damaged part? What about when you get a bacteria or virus, do you tell your lymph nodes to catch potential threats or to send white blood cells to fight infection? We know the answer to these questions. We don't tell our body to do any of these things. It just does. How? Because the truth is "The Power that made the body, heals the body.", as quoted by B.J. Palmer. It doesn't happen any other way. A cardiac surgeon may cut you open and create a bypass so your heart can get the necessary blood it needs. Still, your body has to grow new tissue to make that connection permanent, to heal itself, to repair the damage done to the other parts on the way to the heart such as muscle, skin, and skeleton.

You see, a doctor doesn't fix or heal anything. I'm a doctor, and I'm willing to admit that. We chiropractors, generally speaking, have an understanding that we just remove interference. The body has the innate intelligence to repair, heal, and restore what was lost because of that interference. I don't fix people. I just re-align the joints. That's it. Same with surgeons. They don't fix your heart, knee, or hip. They change it, yes, that's obvious. But the innate intelligence within our bodies sends the cells to protect from infection, the cells for repair and needed proteins to build tissue and more. You don't tell your body to do that, and neither does the doctor. It's your innate intelligence that does that. What an incredible truth, right?!? I think so. I'm genuinely amazed by it. Here's a great story from one of my patients that had interference removed and "the Power that made the body, heal(ed) the body."

I had a patient that gave up on getting pregnant years before coming to me and had adopted a child. She was in her twenties and otherwise perfectly healthy but was experiencing back pain. She was found to have misalignments at several locations throughout her spine, including the lumbar and sacral regions. Following the correction of these vertebrae, the pain she was feeling subsided. I instructed her to return for follow up visits to keep those vertebrae and her sacrum in line. Weeks followed, and she came to me with exciting news, she was pregnant. The only difference she had made in her life was

43

coming to me for chiropractic manipulation. Let's be clear; I did not fix her hormone levels, her ovaries, or her reproductive organs. I also didn't correct her husband's hormone levels. I simply restored proper function to the lumbar and sacral regions, which allowed her reproduction system to be healed and work through the power of the innate intelligence within her body.

There are several case studies of this and other amazing things happening under chiropractic care. One patient received his eyesight back following a chiropractic manipulation and reported it to the news back in 2008. He had been blind in one eye for 12 years. Following a cervical (neck) re-alignment, his blind eye started watering and kept on watering for 45 minutes. Following the watering, his eye had blurry vision and then clear vision. Again, the chiropractor did not fix his eye. He simply removed interference in the cervical region, which was causing dysfunction to some part of the nerves that go to his eye. The man's innate intelligence did the rest. There are cases like these all over the world where restoring innate intelligence and the flow of information from the brain to body parts allowed true healing and repair to take place.

It is because of this fact that the phrase has such power and meaning. Once you realize that The Creator Designed you, you also come to know that it is because of that fact that you can heal yourself, repair yourself, truly fix yourself. A doctor cannot tell your body what to do. It must come from innate intelligence. The Creator gave our bodies everything it needs to maintain what's called homeostasis. Homeostasis is when our bodies are operating as they should; proper temperature, breathing pattern, blood flow, etc., all of our systems working correctly together. He also provided a way for us to repair damaged tissue. The phrase recognizes the power that comes from The Creator. He has such incredible power and wisdom to create our bodies and everything on earth and in the cosmos. What a blessing it is to know that our Creator knows our bodies, its weaknesses, its stresses, its abilities, and everything else. The Creator made us and provided ways for us to fix ourselves truly. Healing indeed doesn't happen any other way.

8

The Gift of Creation

As human beings, The Creator has given us the ability to reproduce. This is the Gift of Creation. He created us and loves us so much that he provided a way for us to procreate and bring life into this world. If you are a parent, you understand how incredible it is to be able to bring a baby into the world. If you are not, please read on to learn about this gift and what you may expect when it is your turn to have this experience.

I can't really describe it. The feeling of love, of the bond you have, of selflessness, is incredible. You instantly feel the desire to do anything in the world for your baby. You know in that moment that you would lay down your life for them. You know that you will do anything you can for that baby to make their life the best you can.

Even if you adopt, you can have that same feeling. It's beautiful. I'm so grateful to my Maker to have been blessed to take a small part in the creation of life. As stated before, I have 3 beautiful children. My wife and I were young when we started. She was 21 and I was 23. We had an incredibly horrible experience with our first born. I'm grateful to be able to share our story with you now.

As a young couple we were excited to start our family. We were married for 5 months when my wife felt the strong desire to have a baby. It was an exciting time. After a little while of trying, The Creator gave us the Gift of Creation. We found out we were expecting just before my dad's birthday. We presented him with a card and announced in the card that he will be getting a grandchild in 9 months. It was so fun. The shock on my sisters face was perfect. We were so happy.

We went to the doctor as normal, had all of our checkups, and followed all of the rules and recommendations. My wife took her vitamins and supplements as suggested as well. The day soon came when we would find out what we were having. It's a boy! We were so happy to hear that he was growing normally and healthily. Not too much later, it was time to start preparing for delivery.

I was working for a fertilization company at the time and the chemicals were considered dangerous. If my wife was to call me at work and say she's going into labor, I would have to go home first and shower then meet her at the hospital. We were talking to the OBGYN about it and she explained that we could plan our birth. We were like, "What?". She explained how she could break the water, give my wife labor inducing meds, and give her an epidural for the pain. This would allow my wife to have a baby without pain and on a schedule so I could be there and not miss it. She explained all of the benefits of it, maybe lightly touched on the risks. With my job and the risk of missing the birth, we opted to schedule an induced labor.

When the day came all appeared to be in order. My wife was laid up in the bed in the standard position (on her back, head and upper body slightly elevated), water broken, drugged up on meds, and was feeling nothing. She ended up falling asleep during labor. I took video and pics and was surprised to see the contractions on the screen but my wife sleeping. It was completely un-natural and didn't feel right at all, but the doctors know what they're doing, right?

My wife did eventually wake up and was clearly not 100% there. The doctor said she was at 10 cm and it's time to push. My wife said, "Push what? I don't feel anything.". The doctor explained that it's like using the bathroom for #2, just push like you would for that. My wife pushed, pushed, and pushed. Every time the doctor said to push with all of her strength my wife did it. She pushed for hours.

Unfortunately our son was stuck in the vaginal canal. We could see his crown but he wouldn't come out. The doctors scared us when they announced that our son was not breathing right and his heart rate was not right. They informed us it was time for a c-section. My wife's fear had been realized. She desperately wanted to experience a vaginal birth and a c-section was the last thing she wanted. The doctor convinced us that we needed to do a c-section now. With a heavy heart, crying in sadness and feeling like a failure, my wife signed the papers.

She was rushed back to the operating room. I was gowned and prepped to be by her side. A blue separation sheet was placed above the belly so my wife and I couldn't see what was going on. Minutes later our baby boy was brought into this world. The doctor held him up for a second for my wife and I to say hello, then immediately over to the newborn station to be cleaned, weighed, pricked, receive his APGAR score, and vaccinated. He was placed in an incubator so he could be supervised to ensure proper vitals. None of this was part of the plan.

Our son was separated from us for hours. My wife was so tired, sad, depressed, and groggy. We started to get upset with the staff. We wanted to see our son! When the night shift nurses came we received a new nurse. This nurse knew the importance of the mother-infant bond. She brought my wife into the newborn unit to touch our sons feet. It was a beautiful moment.

A few hours into the middle of the night the nurse brought our son into the room for us to hold him for the first time. This was 8 hours after he was born. Not at all what we wanted but we were grateful that the time had finally come. The nurse assisted my wife with the breastfeeding process. His innate intelligence was working, mouth puckered, sucking motion initiated, needing no instruction. But the latching process wasn't going as planned. It took longer than expected. It was difficult for my wife but worth it. Our son desperately needed the nutrition from my wife to survive and thrive.

Following a few days in the hospital, my wife was not doing so great. The OBGYN that did the surgery explained that my wife should be doing more and I should be doing less. She discharged us to go home without any meds for my wife or my son. No antibiotics after surgery, no pain killers, nothing.

Within 48 hrs. my wife was spiking a fever. I had to give our son to his grandmother and admit my wife into the hospital since newborns are not allowed into the normal hospital rooms. They had to cut my wife open again and drain an infection that was growing on her uterus from the incision. They did not numb the area adequately enough. She felt extreme pain. Sad part is I was at work when this happened as it was not scheduled to happen until I got there, but they proceeded without me. Over the next couple of days I had to wheel my wife out of the hospital in order for her to see, hold, and feed her newborn son. Now we are upset with the system, the doctor, and everything that has happened.

Once her symptoms subsided and the infection under control, she was released from the hospital. A nurse was scheduled to come by every day to pack her incision. She had absorbent material packed in her and unpacked ever day for 30 days. She also suffered from severe constipation, painful urination, and significant pain. Practically all that could go wrong with a c-section, just shy of losing our child or my wife, went wrong.

We trusted the medical professionals with this experience and it went completely wrong. All of the "benefits" of a scheduled birth were never realized and all of the fears became our reality. The OBGYN stated that my wife had a tilted uterus and the shape of her body would never allow a baby to come out naturally. We originally wanted to have several children. Following that experience I was never going to ask my wife to have another child ever again. My friends and family warned me not to and I agreed. At least our son was healthy, or was he?

Our son had colic, meaning he would cry and cry with no way to please him. We tried every trick in the book and he would not stop crying. It was an extremely difficult time in our parenthood lives. He had all of his routine check ups, vaccines, and follow ups as recommended. He also suffered from ear infection after ear infection. Never seemed to be able to go a time without infection. The pediatrician prescribed antibiotic after antibiotic. The antibiotics ruined his gut, but we didn't know that, and he had severe digestive problems, especially acid reflux in the form of spit up. He spit up on everyone! It became a joke in our family really.

The sad part was he was suffering and the doctors didn't have a single answer. Just cover it up with antibiotics. Just cover it up with drugs. Use a special formula. It must be something we were doing. They had no real reason for our sons condition and no answers. During this time was when I got accepted to chiropractic school. We moved and took our son to Marietta, GA.

Due to the chronic ear infections and lack of development from loss of tone awareness, his pediatrician recommended ear tube surgery. Not again. Before surgery was to take place my wife and I took him to a pediatric chiropractor. Remember, I wasn't raised to believe in chiropractic so this was a little scary. But since we were about to do surgery on our son we figured this couldn't possibly be worse.

Following 2 adjustments that week our son's ears were cleared and he didn't have to go through with the surgery. Whew! What a relief. Following additional adjustments his development started to improve and his ability to hear and speak increased. He started to develop normally.

Once our son was on the right track, to my surprise and everyone else's for that matter, my wife decided she wanted to have another baby. We were blessed to be having a girl this time! We decided to not listen to a single medical doctor throughout the entire process. We went with a midwife nurse instead. My wife received chiropractic adjustments throughout her pregnancy and took her vitamins and supplements as she was supposed to do.

When the time came to prepare for birth, my wife and I wrote up a birthing plan that included no epidural, no meds, no needles, no taking our baby from us from the moment she's born, no vaccines, no drugs, nothing that was not absolutely necessary to save either the life of my wife or our baby girl. We wanted no influence from the medical community at that point. Can you blame us? They pressured and pressured us to have another c-section but we stood our ground. (On a side note, I recommend watching The Business of Being Born, by Ricky Lake. A documentary of how she went through a similar process and was also let down. It reveals a lot about the business of birth and how c-sections, drugs, hormones, induced labors, etc. are big business making a lot of money off of your birth.)

My strong wife, following a few hours of labor, walking back and forth, squatting, going on all fours, and moving around to positions she felt were comfortable, was able to have a VBAC. This is also known as a vaginal birth after c-section, and our beautiful baby daughter was born. She went straight up to my wife's chest and was cleaned right there. We left the umbilical cord in tact for over a minute, allowing more nutrient rich blood to be passed onto our daughter. We got to hold her, feel her, stare at her, and love on her. My wife was able to start breastfeeding right away. This was the dream of bringing a baby into this world. This was the way our Maker wanted us to have children. It felt right. It felt good. It was an incredible experience.

Our daughter didn't have colic, infections, digestion issues, or health issues of any kind. Our third child was like the second. Another successful vaginal birth to a healthy daughter. She too received no medications, no needles, no vaccines, and never had colic, infections, digestion issues, or health issues of any kind. We have been truly blessed. I'm grateful to be able to take a small part in allowing our children to grow up with their Innate Intelligence functioning at optimum levels. They know the importance of keeping their body healthy, keeping it in line as to not alter the flow of information from brain to body, and yes, even drinking plenty of water.

The Creator designed our bodies. He designed the entire birthing process. He knows how it's supposed to go. If you believe this with 100% certainty, as many of you do in the world, why do we place so much trust in man? Why don't we trust the design The Creator has given us? As stated earlier, more often than not, our body doesn't need outside influence, just no interference. If we let the body do what

The Creator designed it to do and only intervene when absolutely necessary, wouldn't that make more sense than intervening all of the time?

Birth is supposed to be an incredible experience. Painful? Yes! Worth it? Yes! So many women are scared to have natural childbirth. So many are scared to even try a vaginal birth with or without an epidural. Several are opting for a scheduled c-section due to the ease of scheduling it and not having to go through the pain and suffering of childbirth. This is not The Creator's way. This is not what you were designed to be able to do. You are capable of so much more! Research it for yourself. Don't jump to an uneducated decision like my wife and I did. Regardless of your decision, I pray you have a healthy baby full of life and a healthy mommy too.

On a side note, if you are not able to have children, my heart goes out to you. I pray you receive comfort during those times you wish you could have a child of your own. As you know, there are options out there. Find out how you can bless the lives of babies at hospitals, at daycare facilities, and more. Research what it takes to adopt if you are able and capable. There are so many babies that are in need of a loving parent in this world. Go, find a baby to love. It could be a niece, a nephew, a baby in the NICU, a foster child, a grandchild, and so on. They need you! You can still use the gifts The Creator gave you to bless the lives of babies and children. Bless you!

Facts about vaginal vs. c-section birth and babies:

1. C-section rates were never supposed to go above 15% in any developed country, yet in America we are at 33%.[1]
2. C-section babies are less likely to have skin-to-skin contact following birth.[1] (We are evidence of that!)
3. Vaginal birth allows the mother-infant bond to be created right away, which has several health benefits, including breathing regulation, heartbeat regulation, metabolic adaptation, and stabilization of blood glucose levels.[1]
4. C-section babies are at higher risk for respiratory illness, including asthma and allergies.[1]
5. Infant respiratory distress syndrome, a complication related to scheduled c-sections, was the most expensive condition of all hospital stays in 2005.[1]
6. Normal labor allows the baby to be squeezed during contractions that prepare the baby's lungs for respiration at birth.[1]
7. Catecholamines which help your baby preserve oxygen stores, adapt to lower oxygen levels, and absorb excess fluid in the lungs are lower in a c-section baby than a vaginally born baby.[1]
8. Planned c-sections have 3x the risk of losing their baby in the first 4 weeks of life as compared to vaginal birth. 3x![1]
9. A vaginal birth squeezes fluid out of the baby's lungs. That process reduces the incidence of breathing problems for the baby.[2]
10. During vaginal birth, the baby receives a helpful dose of good bacteria. This helps boost the baby's immune system and protects the intestinal tract.[2]

References:

1. April 18, 2016. How Does a Cesarean Affect the Baby? <vbac.com>.
2. Martin, LuVerda C. November 21, 2017. What's the Difference? Natural Delivery or C-section. <aurorahealthcare.org>.

If you had to have a c-section as we did. Or if you had to do it for another reason, my heart goes out to you as well. It's not your fault. You didn't do anything wrong. If the doctor told you it's your fault because your body isn't right and never will be, don't believe it! See a chiropractor and see if that can change your body's structure if necessary. I hope your baby isn't suffering from any of the above problems, or problems like my son had. If they are, I encourage you to seek alternative treatments. They worked for my son and could work for your child too. If you elected to have a c-section and all worked out just fine, I'm happy for you and your baby. I want all mothers to have a successful birth, whatever that may end up being, but above all, I want all mothers and babies to be healthy and full of life. I especially want all babies to have the best opportunity at a healthy life, and hopefully, this chapter will help that become a reality for thousands of parents out there.

9

You have been given a Gift, Give if You Can

Give if You Can. The Creator gave you everything you are. He provided your entire frame, your blood, your organs, your intellect, all of it. This gift is free to you. You don't have to do anything to earn this gift. It is yours automatically. It is because He loves us so much that He wants us to have this body. He wants us to be able to experience life on this Earth to the best that we can.

Congratulations, you have one of the biggest blessings you'll ever receive in your existence. If you have two eyes that can see, two ears that can hear, two arms with functioning hands, two legs with functioning feet, functioning systems in your body, you have A LOT to be grateful for. I hope that you thank your Creator daily for those blessings.

For those of you reading this that are missing parts, are experiencing disease, are not functioning normally, and not able to see, or hear, or touch, or more. You are not alone. You are not cursed for some reason. The Creator does not curse your body. As stated earlier, your body may be different and handicapped due to interference in the innate intelligence, in the genes, in the cells, but that does not define you.

He didn't do that to you to punish you or your parents. He allows these side effects, these adverse reactions, these gene problems, to create a unique mix of people on this beautiful Earth He created. Some religious texts teach us that you cannot truly appreciate good without experiencing some of the bad. You cannot truly appreciate being pain-free unless you experience pain. Same with appreciating any of your body parts.

Ever sprain an ankle, wrist, shoulder, hip? Ever pull a muscle? When you lose the function of those parts, you gain a little appreciation for that part once you have it back. I hear patients complain about their lives and their struggles every day. Some share everything about their lives, often too much info. But for those that are chronic complainers, I often remind them that someone else out there is going through similar obstacles and suffering. Many are far worse.

Everyone needs to have the proper perspective to appreciate this amazing gift truly. One of the most influential and positive people I know is paralyzed from the waist down. How can he be so happy? How can he do so much with a smile on his face when he is in a wheelchair? Because he is grateful for what he does have.

He knows The Creator loves him. He loves The Creator and expresses gratitude for the blessings he has. Something my kids could tell you is one of my favorite phrases, "Have an attitude of gratitude." Be grateful for your blessings, someone out there has it worse, I promise.

Now let's say you are healthy, you take care of this Gift of the Human Body you have received from The Creator, and you appreciate it. You eat right. You exercise. You do what you can to maintain it in a way that allows your body systems to function at optimum. What can you do to Give if You Can?

I am grateful to my Creator. I have been blessed with a healthy body. The Creator has allowed my body to be whole, complete, and to come from a good gene pool. These factors have allowed me to be blessed tremendously, and I never wanted to take that for granted. He blessed me to have O- blood, the "Universal Donor" blood type, just like my father. I also felt as if The Creator wanted me to use this gift to bless the lives of others. So I do.

I donate blood as often as the schedule for donating allows, just as my father has most of his life. I'll donate a double red blood cell amount if I have the time. I signed up to be an organ donor, so if The Creator decides to take me while I'm healthy, my organs can be used to save a life or give someone a fighting chance at life. I believe it is my social responsibility to give what I can when I can. I have signed up to be a bone marrow donor, so hopefully, I can save a life that needs bone marrow. I hope this doesn't come across as boasting. That is not my intention. I'm trying to give you examples of what you can do, and what I believe you should do if you are blessed with a healthy body, a healthy gene pool, and good blood. There is so much we can do to bless the lives of others using the gift The Creator gave us.

Give if You Can. Give blood, give an organ, give bone marrow, give money if you have extra, give a helping hand in times of need. We can give by touring nursing homes, hospitals, and retirement homes and using our bodies to deliver happiness and joy to others. We can go to food banks, soup kitchens, and other facilities to use our bodies to help others in need. You can volunteer at one of many different organizations that can allow you to use your body to bless others.

I'm grateful for the opportunities I have had with "Helping Hands," an organization that is a part of The Church of Jesus Christ of Latter-Day Saints. Wearing the yellow shirt uniform, I have taken part in disaster relief efforts and clean up efforts following every major disaster that has hit Florida in the last decade. It has been an honor to use this body, this gift from The Creator, to bless the lives of others. I implore you. I encourage you. I plead with you. Use what you have been blessed with and Give if You Can.

10

The Gift of Love

I had to include a chapter about Love. Why? Because love is the most powerful emotional connection we can have or experience during this life. The Creator gave it to us as a sample of what is possible. The incredible part about it is that The Creator loves us more than we can comprehend. He loves us so much that he gave us this body, this earth, this universe, and everything in-between. He gave us a body like He has. He made us after His likeness, to be just like Him. He allows us to experience life, the good and the bad, the darkness and the light, so we can have joy.

As stated earlier, we cannot fully appreciate something without experiencing the opposite of it. When we have our heartbroken, when we feel abandoned, when we feel all is lost, we can look to the heavens and cry unto our Maker. We can then feel found; we can feel a connection; we can feel of His love.

Love Yourself

Loving yourself is kind of like preparing for retirement. You have to pay yourself first a little; then you can pay for this, that, and the other. If you don't love yourself, you are going to find it very difficult to love someone else, to trust someone, or to create connections. You are a child of The Creator. He made you to be different from all others on earth that have lived, are living, or ever will live. There will never be another you. You are so special!

But He cannot make you love yourself. You have to do that. You need to set aside time for yourself. You need to do something for you every once in a while. But that doesn't suggest you should be selfish. You can go and do something for a stranger. Go volunteer and serve others. You'll gain a love for yourself and be able to pat yourself on the back.

There are a lot of great ways to gain a love for yourself. The problem is that there are just as many ways to lose that love. Remember the step in Chapter 5 about getting away from a negative environment or negative people? People will hurt you. Loved ones may let you down and cause you to feel worthless. Haters are going to hate. There is one constant, The Creator's love for you.

He will never leave you. He knows everything you're going through. He knows your pain. He knows your suffering. He knows your loss. He also knows how to lift you up when you are down. He knows what makes you happy and brings joy into your life. Seek Him. Once you find Him, you will never be alone. Once you realize that you are special and love yourself, you can truly bless the lives of others with that love.

<u>Love Others</u>

If you look into most religions, they call on you to love your neighbor. In The Holy Bible, one of the Ten Commandments is to love your neighbor as yourself. Now, if you lack in love for yourself, how can you truly love your neighbor? That's why love of yourself is so important. It comes before love for others. How can you show The Creator that you love your neighbors? There are many ways to do this.

If you are already doing service and helping others as often as you can, great! Continue down that path and bless the lives of others. If you haven't done this type of thing before, start small. Hold a door open for a stranger. Offer a hand to a person trying to load a lot of groceries into their trunk. Randomly call a loved one and see how they're doing. Once you get comfortable and notice how you feel about doing this, there will be a drive inside you to do more. You can serve others in so many ways.

The Creator says in many religious scriptures that when we are serving others, it is as if we are serving Him. How incredible, right?!?! We show our love and gratitude to our

Maker by serving others. Simple! It might not be easy, but it's simple. Go and serve. You'll be so happy you did.

Love for others and The Creator has driven me to do so much throughout my life. I'm so grateful to have the opportunity I have to bless the lives of others through service. From offering free treatment to those who cannot afford it to helping cut up a tree that has fallen on a neighbors property. I love to serve. Teaching my children to do this has been so rewarding that it cannot be put into words.

Watching them shop for underprivileged children and saying, "I want the little girl to have this, daddy!" with a huge smile on their faces lights up my life. Watching my son make trip after trip carrying debris after a hurricane destroyed someone's property brings me joy beyond measure. If you have children, teach them and allow them to serve others.

Help them come up with ways to serve your neighbors. You will feel what it's like when The Creator sees us serving others. You will get a glimpse of the joy and pride that He has for you when you serve others. It is truly a passion in my life, and I'm grateful to have been raised to be this way. (Thank you mom and dad! Your example has made my life full of love and joy!)

Love Your Creator

How do we show love to The Creator? How do we let Him know that we are grateful for our own lives? Well, we can start by taking the steps in Chapter 5. That will put you on the right track. Loving yourself and your neighbors is also extremely important. According to The Holy Bible and everyone in the Christian world, they are expected to first and foremost love God with all of their heart, might, mind, and strength. Why would it be first? I believe it is because without loving The Creator, there is no loving ourselves or our neighbors. Some of you that don't believe in a Creator are calling me out on this right about now. You argue that you love yourself and your neighbors and don't believe in a higher power, so my argument is lost. Allow me to explain.

What is love? How can you explain it? You can't. Yet you probably use that word to convey a connection you have with a loved one, a friend, a food, a drink, etc. What does it mean? Where does it come from? What is in us that possesses us to be willing to do practically anything for it? Why would a person take a bullet for a total stranger? Why would a person take time away from their own lives and serve others? Why show love to those that hate us? Why be kind to those that are mean to us and hurt us? Why?

Science cannot explain any of these questions. Science cannot explain the true nature of love. There are facts about love, but no one knows why we have it. The "Why?" is the big question here. The Creator gave us Love because He wants us to experience a little bit of what He has for us. He gave us the Gift of Love because He loves us beyond comprehension. That is why science cannot figure it out. It makes more sense to me to believe that love is given to us. It is innate, inborn, natural. It is powerful, beyond science powerful.

<u>Some fun facts about love:</u>

1. When a person is "in love" with another person, dopamine production is increased in the brain. Similar to when a person is addicted to cocaine. The good news is that dopamine production from love is harmless.
2. When you cuddle with a loved one, you trigger the release of oxytocin. It relaxes you and makes you feel good. It can even help reduce pain and headaches.
3. There's a syndrome called "Broken Heart Syndrome", which is when a person experiences a broken heart from a loss, a break-up, or betrayal, and suffers from pain and shortness of breath, which can be misdiagnosed as a heart attack.
4. People in the early stages of love produce lower levels of serotonin, which is associated with happiness levels, and higher levels of cortisol, which is associated with stress levels. It is similar to Obsessive-Compulsive Disorder, which explains why someone may feel obsessed with another.
5. Expressing gratitude towards those you love will cause an immediate spike in happiness levels.
6. A 75-year-long study by Harvard found that patient's happiness and life fulfillment almost exclusively revolved around love. More than wealth, more than health, it was the pursuit of love that predicted well-being.
7. People with higher self-esteem tend to have longer, more successful relationships.
8. Merely looking at a picture of a loved one can have pain-killing effects.

9. The urge to fall in love is a biological drive we are born with.
10. Health benefits of being in love and being loved are countless.

Reference: Steven Y. 42 Lovely Facts About Love. <factinate.com>

The Gift of Love is the most incredible of all the emotions the Human Body can possess. It is the closest thing to feeling what The Creator feels for each of us. Crazy part is His love for us is way more powerful and encompassing than anything else we can experience. Participating in the creation of life and feeling that love for our children is probably the closest we can get. Some argue that it's when you have grandchildren. I don't know about that yet. I can only say this, that The Creator loves you and me. He loves us all. He has given me more than I deserve. He is my maker, and I am grateful to Him for all of the blessings in my life. Love others. Love yourself. Spread love to all you come in contact with.

11

Respect the Design

Hopefully, by now you are convinced that you were Designed by The Creator. Hopefully, you have a new found love and respect for that creation, which is you. You are special. You are unique. You were designed exactly the way you were meant to be. All of your imperfections, weaknesses, strengths, will, and desire.

Remember, He created you in His image. The Creator gave this body to you as a gift. Your job is to take care of that gift and treasure it. Don't willingly do things to it that make it appear that you are ungrateful for this gift. As is common with most religious sects, The Creator expects us to treat our bodies a certain way, and there are consequences if we don't.

If we decide that our bodies are indeed ours, not a gift from a Creator, we may feel that we should be able to do whatever we want to it. We may feel the desire to eat, drink, and be merry for tomorrow we die, a common phrase taken from multiple verses in The Holy Bible. We may feel that we should take up habits that could hurt or destroy our bodies. We may participate in activities that show complete disregard for the safety of our bodies. This is up to us. We have the power to do what we want to our bodies, but there will be consequences.

Those that drink too much end up with a toxic liver that may be damaged beyond repair and could lead to death. Those that smoke too much end up with damaged lungs, again sometimes damaged beyond repair leading to cancer and possibly death. Those that love tattoos, sun tanning, and other methods of changing their skin, can do too much that may lead to problems with their skin, including infections or cancer. As you can see, the consequences of disrespecting our bodies can be fatal.

So how do we respect the design? By treating it well. By making sure it has all it needs to be in tip-top shape. We need to eat the right things and have a balanced diet. We need to drink plenty of water. Yes, I'm stressing the importance of water again. Water is an essential part of all cells in our bodies. Most of us do not drink nearly enough. I recommend a gallon a day for total hydration and cleanliness. If you're a child or otherwise not able too, a half gallon a day would be good.

We should exercise if possible. Those of you that believe you are not able, ask yourself truthfully, "Am I able to exercise?". A common phrase I hear from my patients is that "I'm too old.". I always bring up the senior Olympics and senior weightlifters, such as the over 80 weightlifting competition. Most are in shock to hear of those folks in their 80's pumping iron. Truth is most can do some form of exercise. Some extremely fit individuals I know are in a wheelchair or paralyzed in an arm, a leg, or worse. They have many reasons not to exercise, but they do it anyway. These few simple lifestyle changes are a great way to show The Creator that we love and respect the design He provided for us.

We can also appreciate the design by recognizing the power that is in it. Remember the chapter on Sick or Healthy? We show respect to The Creator by not being quick to intervene with medications that cover up symptoms. When we are suffering from a symptom, we can try to understand why we are having that symptom. What is my innate intelligence trying to tell me about what is wrong in my body? Maybe it's the way I have been treating it? Perhaps it's what I've been eating?

We also show respect by learning more about the natural body processes and systems that are in place to take care of our amazing bodies. Learn more about them. Study them. The complexities and miracles inside the human body, your body, will amaze you. After all, it was Designed by The Creator. I love and appreciate you for taking the time to read this book. I hope it has convinced you that you were Designed by The Creator.

CONCLUSION

In conclusion, I hope you have learned something about you. I hope that you understand how beautiful and lovely you are just as you are now. I hope that you know that your body is a gift from The Creator. Hopefully, I have proven that fact to you. You should now know, if you didn't before, what you can be doing to release the flow of innate intelligence within you. Remember to take the steps discussed in Chapter 5. These steps will help you achieve optimum innate intelligence flow and proper communication from the brain to organ/part/tissue/cell. I know that The Creator Designed my body and yours. I know that the human species was not evolved from anything on this earth. It was a gift given to us by our Maker. He designed us after His image. It is truly a fantastic gift. I'm grateful for it, and hopefully, you are too. Thank you for reading Designed by The Creator: The Human Body and the Innate Intelligence Within, I truly enjoyed writing it.

Sincerely,

Curtis Reynolds, D.C.

I CHALLENGE YOU

If you still aren't sure about The Creator, or God as I call Him, I challenge you. I challenge you to get on your knees and bow before your maker. I challenge you to pray to Him with real intent and a broken heart. Talk to Him. Share your problems with Him. Express gratitude for the blessings in your life. If you humbly do this, I know you can receive His love and the feeling of His peace and comfort all around you. It might take several tries or several minutes, even hours. Days can pass by and then something happens. Could be an interaction with a person. Could be when you're alone or meditating. Sometimes people describe it like it hit them like a ton of bricks. Others describe it as a still small voice. You feel Him. You feel this power around you that you cannot fully describe. If you feel that, you know He's real. You know He's listening and He's there for you. You know He created you. You'll know, without a doubt, that He loves you. You'll know, as I do, that you were Designed by The Creator.

About the Author:

Dr. Curtis Reynolds is a husband, father, Christian, humanitarian, and entrepreneur. As a Doctor of Chiropractic, he has studied the human body and has treated patients for over a decade. He has used his gifts as a Chiropractor to help patients as young as a day old and patients up to 94 years old. He has helped thousands achieve better health over the course of his career. He's currently the owner of ChiroMed Health Spa with 3 locations in Manatee County, FL, and Elite Integrated Medical Centers in Ellenton, FL (opening summer of 2020). He also has an invention in the works to protect both doctor and patient in the healthcare industry.

He's the fifth of six children, and was raised by loving parents Debbie and Carl. He was brought up in and is a member of The Church of Jesus Christ of Latter Day Saints. He achieved the rank of Eagle Scout, the highest achievement in scouts. He has attended school in 4 states, including Hawaii, and has three college Degrees. He loves doing outdoor activities like camping, hiking, biking, and others but he especially loves fishing. He also enjoys dancing, singing, and baking. He loves playing sports of all kinds but basketball is his favorite. Above all else, he loves spending time with his family.

He enjoys the opportunity he has to use the blessings he has received to bless the lives of others. Dr. Reynolds offers free chiropractic care to those that can't afford it, is involved in charitable organizations, and volunteers as often as he can. He helps people change their lives for the better with diet counseling, exercise counseling, chiropractic care, and physical therapy. He has volunteered to serve in different capacities at his local church including leadership and youth leadership positions. He hopes to bless the lives of others using books to bring hope, peace, love, and kindness to the world.

You can reach out to him via email at:
DrReynolds@DrCurtisReynolds.com

Or by mail:
Dr. Reynolds Books
723 7th St W
Palmetto, FL

If you live in the greater Tampa Bay area and you're interested in being a patient of Dr. Reynolds please call 941-479-4999. His amazing staff will get you in as quickly as possible.

God bless you all!